Original title:
The Fiddle-Leaf Files

Copyright © 2025 Creative Arts Management OÜ
All rights reserved.

Author: Robert Ashford
ISBN HARDBACK: 978-1-80581-902-8
ISBN PAPERBACK: 978-1-80581-429-0
ISBN EBOOK: 978-1-80581-902-8

In the Embrace of Petals

In a pot where secrets hide,
A plant decided to confide.
With leaves that danced in the breeze,
It told tales of wobbly knees.

Spiders spun webs, quite the show,
Leaves giggled, putting on a glow.
Whispers of nature, oh so divine,
A flower blushed, call it benign.

Midnight Gardens of Reflection

At the stroke of twelve, plants did sway,
In moonlight's glow, they joined the play.
With roots in gossip, they would shout,
What secrets do ferns feel without a doubt?

A rogue sunflower donned a hat,
Stretched its stalk, imagine that!
The daisies rolled in laughter's grip,
As shadows twirled in a leafy trip.

Leafy Dialogues

A cactus said, "I'm feeling prickly!"
While ferns replied, "We love you fickly."
In chatty pots, the herbs convened,
"Do our jokes need more verdant genes?"

With basil bold and parsley sly,
They plotted a date: "Bring the chive!"
In leafy banter, joy took flight,
They giggled till dawn's early light.

Chronicles of Hidden Greenery

Underneath the soil, they scheme,
Roots with dreams of a greener theme.
A tale of growth, a struggle grand,
For sunlight's kiss, they stretch their hand.

Sneaky snails with plans so slick,
Translate leaves with just one flick.
They crack jokes on the way to bloom,
And share potluck in the room.

The Language of Photosynthesis

In the sun's warm embrace, they sway,
Leaves whisper secrets of the day.
Chlorophyll sings in vibrant hues,
Tickling the air with playful views.

Roots play tag beneath the soil,
Gathering nutrients, their daily toil.
A circle of life with laughter so sweet,
Nature's ballet, an elegant feat.

Dance of the Verdant Spirits

In a forest of green, they swirl and spin,
Petals in twirls, let the fun begin.
The branches are giggling, a fluttering crowd,
As breezes bring laughter, crisp and loud.

With vines interlaced, the party's on,
Dancing till dusk, till the last light's gone.
The grasses hum tunes, a merry refrain,
Join in the dance, let go of the mundane.

An Exhale of Chlorophyll

Gasping for air, in a laughable way,
Plants breathe out joy, come what may.
Oxygen bubbles, a hiccup and pop,
Nature's own humor, we can't make it stop!

With roots in the ground, they chuckle and cheer,
Every green leaf brings good vibes near.
In the world of plants, where laughter is loud,
Mirth is the oxygen, nature's own shroud.

Green Veins and Moonlight

Under moonlight's glow, leaves shimmer bright,
Green veins glow softly in the night.
A chatty fern tells jokes to the trees,
While crickets join in with chirps on the breeze.

The night air chuckles, filled with delight,
As shadows dance under the starry light.
Nature's own comedy, a show to behold,
In the kingdom of green, where laughter unfolds.

Secrets Under the Leafy Canopy

In the shade, a squirrel dances,
Claiming acorns like a king.
Whispers from the leafy branches,
Strange tales that trees might sing.

A raccoon wears a scarf so neat,
Pretends to be a great chef.
Leaves giggle beneath its feet,
As it makes a mess, no doubt left!

With every rustle, secrets shared,
Beneath the boughs, a gossip stream.
Tales of droughts and storms declared,
Life's a leafy, silly dream!

The Breeze of Forgotten Flora

Breezes bring us stories old,
Of flowers that danced in the breeze.
Petals bright with tales untold,
Now they just sneeze and wheeze!

Once a daisy wore a hat,
Claiming it was all the rage.
But now it's just a scruffy brat,
Lying down in leaf's green cage.

Whimsical weeds wear crowns of dust,
Pretending to be royalty.
Yet all they do is fade and rust,
In this game of foliage folly!

Traces of Enchantment

Among the leaves, the gnomes do play,
   Crafting mischief with delight.
   Hiding socks and hearts away,
Making nighttime bloom so bright.

A toadstool hosts a tiny feast,
   With acorn caps as fancy plates.
   Laughter spills, not one but least,
As fireflies toast to silly fates!

Sprinkled dust of magic hidden,
   Twinkling brightly in the night.
Nature's pranks, oh, who are bidden,
   To join this whimsical, wild flight?

Journeys Through Leafy Lanes

Walking down the shady lane,
A hedgehog hums a cheerful tune.
"Step aside!" the cat proclaims,
"This journey's mine from noon to moon!"

Tangled vines with giggles weave,
Each turn a playful twist or bend.
Where do foliage fairies grieve?
In puddles, they hop and pretend!

Oh the paths of green delight,
A slip, a trip, then laughter loud.
Underneath the stars so bright,
We sing and dance, a silly crowd!

Chronicles from a Leafy Veil

In a room where plants hold court,
A leaf once tried to play a sport.
It rolled and tumbled, much to glee,
But fell flat, much like a tree.

A spider spun a grand ballet,
While snails debated night and day.
The fern just sighed, laid back with flair,
Saying, "This place needs more fresh air!"

The cacti cracked a prickly joke,
While orchids spun a fragrant poke.
With every leaf, a giggle grew,
In this green tale, all felt anew.

So gather round, both big and small,
In leafy halls we dance and sprawl.
With every twist, we laugh and cheer,
In this green kingdom, there's no fear.

Beneath the Verdant Veil

In a port where petals plot and scheme,
A shrub proposed a wild ice cream.
The roses blushed, their colors bright,
While daisies cheered with sheer delight.

The vines began a prank or two,
They twirled around a squirrel or two.
With each twist, the laughter spread,
A dance of leaves, all lightly tread.

A rogue fern wore a funny hat,
A trendy look, how about that?
With every glance, the giggles grew,
In our green world, it's all brand new.

So raise a leaf, let stories soar,
In this lush realm, who could ask for more?
With every bloom, the fun's alive,
In nature's play, we all can thrive.

Tales from the Verdant Arch

Once beneath the leafy shade,
A cucumber tried a waltz parade.
It tripped and fell, so loud a thud,
Creating quite the veggie flood.

A petal painted with a grin,
Declared, "Now let the fun begin!"
They tossed some seeds in jubilee,
And watched them sprout with joyful glee.

An acorn shared a goofy riddle,
While mossy mates played an odd fiddle.
With laughter ringing through the grove,
Each tale told made the antics strove.

So in this arch of green and gold,
The stories bloom, both brave and bold.
With humor loud, we plant our roots,
In this verdant world, wear funky boots!

The Silent Symphony of Foliage

In a world of leaves, quite silent, true,
A beetle brought a drum or two.
With every beat, the branches swayed,
While dancing leaves and laughter played.

A dandelion with puffs so light,
Joined in the fun, a sheer delight.
It blew its seeds both far and wide,
Creating chaos, laughter, pride.

The rhododendron, with petals wide,
Wore shades of pink, oh what a ride!
It chuckled deep, its joy so real,
In this green space, we all can feel.

So sway along, let nature sing,
In leafy lore, there's joy to bring.
With every note, let laughter flow,
Together in this leafy show.

The Secrets of Sunlit Corners

In a pot near the window, a plant takes a stance,
It stretches for sunlight, engaging in dance.
A cat walks by, gives a curious stare,
That leafy green giant just doesn't care.

With leaves like umbrellas, they catch every ray,
Whispering secrets of a bright, leafy day.
While dust bunnies gather in corners so tight,
That plant's living large, it's feeling just right.

Tales from the Lush Canopy

High up in the leaves, a squirrel plots fun,
He dreams of acorns and a race to outrun.
The plants laugh together, all swaying with glee,
As the critters below sip on cups of sweet tea.

When the rain falls down, they do a quick jig,
Each drop is a dance, it's a glorious gig.
While the world below grumbles and rushes along,
The leafy elite serenade with their song.

Bask in the Leafy Glow

In each sunny beam, the leaves bask and gleam,
They shoot silly glances, like part of a dream.
A little ladybug joins in for a chat,
Complaining of snails who just won't take that spat.

The sun's golden rays are a grand comedy,
As plants take their bows, just wild and free.
While there's noise all around, they stay quite aloof,
Judging houseplants' hairstyles, who needs a goof?

Resilience in the Green Veins

A leaf with a curl shows off its great flair,
While others look on with a green sort of stare.
They giggle and gossip about who grows best,
While someone is pulling out weeds as a jest.

In a world full of drama, they keep it all light,
Throwing shade on the neighbors, it's all in good spite.
With jokes in their veins and soil as their throne,
Those plants are the wildest, yet stand all alone.

In Search of the Perfect Leaf

I wandered through jungles of potted delight,
Searching for greens that could dance in the light.
Some leaves were too crispy, some far too serene,
A leaf with a wink? Now that would be keen!

I asked a tall cactus, 'Have you seen any flair?'
He shrugged with a grin, 'Not a leaf in the air.'
I tickled a fern, with a curious poke,
It giggled and whispered, 'You'll find what you soak.'

Roots Buried in Daydreams

In soil of my fantasies, roots took their flight,
They stretched for a donut, and settled in tight.
The dreams are all tasty, with toppings galore,
But these visions of munchies leave me wanting more!

My roots whisper jokes from the depths of the earth,
They chortle and chuckle, in for what it's worth.
I'm often just giggling, swaying with glee,
While the plants roll their eyes, 'Oh dear, here comes she!'

Drifting Through Canopies

I drift through the leaves like a butterfly friend,
But most of my landing just seems to offend.
A leaf with a giggle, a trunk full of cheer,
I stumble through branches, forget what brought me here.

A sloth gives a nod, with a slow, lazy blink,
While a parrot squawks nonsense, or so I think.
The sunlight is painting, a picture of smiles,
As I fumble through forests, and trip on my trials.

Heartbeats of the Nature Muse

The trees keep on rustling, a bard with no rhyme,
They sway to the music of my silly climb.
But nature's a muse, with a humor so sly,
It tickles the green with a breezy goodbye.

The flowers all giggle as I lose my way,
I'm caught in a blossom; now what will I say?
They whisper sweet nonsense, with petals that sway,
Reminding me gently, it's fine not to play.

Secrets in the Canopy

In the greenery above, whispers reside,
Mischievous leaves, secrets they hide.
A squirrel steals snacks, what a bold feat,
While the wise old owl keeps time with a beat.

Dancing in shadows, the branches sway,
Chatting with breezes throughout the day.
The roots hold stories only they know,
While ants debate where the next picnic goes.

A flower chuckles, spreading its cheer,
While ferns exchange gossip—oh what a year!
With every rustle, a tale unwinds,
Nature's comedy, leaving us in smiles behind.

So tiptoe through laughter, as sunlight spills,
Amongst nature's wonders and playful thrills.
The world above teems with whimsical fate,
Secrets in the canopy, don't be late!

Echoes of Earthy Elegance

A cactus dons shades, looking quite bright,
While daisies gossip about their last flight.
Moss gets tickled by a playful breeze,
And Tansy the cat prances with ease.

The sunflowers wink, with heads held up high,
They wave to the clouds passing on by.
Whispers of laughter in the petals abound,
As roots dance below in the soft, rich ground.

A beetle in bow ties tips his hat,
And ladybugs giggle, how charming is that?
Fungi in flapper dresses twirl in delight,
Earthy elegance blooms, almost too bright!

Nature teems with charm, a playful parade,
Each leaf has a punchline, nature's charade.
In this realm of flora, joyful and free,
Echoes of laughter fill up every tree.

Treetop Chronicles

High above the world, in a leafy round,
Squirrels share tales, making quite the sound.
The breeze is a bard with stories to tell,
Of goofy geometry where branches fell.

A parrot declares, "I'll outsing the flock!"
While chipmunks conspire by the bumpy rock.
They giggle and joke, in their feathered coats,
While the moon listens close to their tiny notes.

Pine cones drop jewels, underfoot they lay,
While laughter erupts—their playful ballet.
A raccoon with sass steals the spotlight away,
In this treetop theater, come what may!

Chronicles written in bark and in leaves,
Funny and quirky, as each season weaves.
With nature's delight, we dance in this place,
Treetop tales hide a smile on each face.

The Dance of Botanical Dreams

In a garden of giggles, the daisies prance,
With petals that flutter, causing a glance.
Their roots, they hum songs, so merry and bright,
While the moon plays the flute, laughing in delight.

Vines twist and twirl, in a botanical spin,
A cheeky bud whispers, 'Oh let's begin!'
The tulips are swaying, hand in green hand,
As the grass stands up, forming a band.

The broccoli breaks out in a funky jam,
While cucumbers chuckle, "Oh, this is the plan!"
Lettuce looks dapper, in its leafy tux,
As tomatoes swing low with a punch and a whack.

So join in the fun, in this garden of dreams,
Where laughter is woven in sunshine beams.
The dance of green whimsy, in nature's embrace,
Botanical memories, how sweet is this place!

The Pulse of Nature's Heart

In the pot, a plant does sway,
With leaves that dance, they laugh and play.
Water them once, or maybe twice,
They'll thrive on love, not just precise.

Roots deep down, they plot and scheme,
Whispering secrets, you wouldn't dream.
A jungle gym for bugs galore,
While I just wonder, what's in store?

Each leaf a meme, a living jest,
They poke at sunlight, do their best.
When dusk arrives, they all retreat,
In leafy pajamas, oh what a treat!

Nature's pulse in vibrant hues,
Winking at me, like it's in the news.
With soil and sun, we've got a pact,
In this green world, joy's an act!

The Embrace of Verdant Buds

In every corner, green buds peek,
Whispering tales, oh so unique.
A shot of sun, a splash of rain,
Their quirky charm keeps me sane.

Cactus chuckles, flowers winks,
While leafy pals share glances, blinks.
A garden party, just us ferns,
With little dance moves, life adjourns.

Sprouts that giggle when raindrops fall,
Nature's laughter, it enchants all.
Petals confetti in summer's breeze,
Forming smiles, just with ease.

Branches sway like they know a joke,
Nature's punchlines in fragrant smoke.
With every sprout, a tale retold,
In this embrace, lives unfold!

Poems of Petals and Serenity

Petals flutter, soft and sweet,
Like tiny dancers on their feet.
In the breeze, they chase the sun,
With giggles that could make one run.

Lilies gossip and tulips tease,
As nature hums a tune with ease.
Each bud a chapter, a tale anew,
In blooms of laughter, joy shines through.

In gardens bright, the mischief flows,
With sneaky scents, like little prose.
The bees all buzz in their funny suits,
Pollinating giggles, sprouting roots.

Calm and laughter hand in hand,
As greenery creates a grand stand.
For in each petal, a secret beams,
In this serene play, nature dreams!

The Enigma of Leafy Silence

In leafy silence, whispers grow,
Tickling secrets that they know.
A rustle here, a sway, a sigh,
Nature's humor, oh me, oh my!

Underneath the moonlit glow,
Cacti plotting, putting on a show.
They giggle softly, share a snort,
In this jungle, laughter's sport.

Every leaf holds a funny face,
In stillness, they find their space.
As shadows stretch, they tell a tale,
Of pollen parties and adventurous trails.

And when the wind begins to dance,
The branches join in, take the chance.
In leafy silence, jokes take flight,
While all around, gentle twilight!

Shadows of Flora Dwell

In corners where the sunlight plays,
A plant begins its dance of praise.
With leaves like fans, it sways and bends,
Pretending to be friends with trends.

A shadow lurks with cheeky glee,
Mocking plants that wish to be free.
It whispers secrets, tales of lore,
Of how to stand out, or be ignored.

The soil below chuckles with mirth,
For every sprout knows its worth.
A leap of faith, a growing spree,
In the greenest realm, there's no decree.

So tip your hat to leaves so bright,
In sunlit days and starry night.
In shadows soft and whispers of cheer,
The joy of plants is always near.

Soliloquy of the Leaf

A leaf took stage to share its tale,
Of rainy days and winds that wail.
It sighed of times it danced with glee,
And once got stuck in a friendly tree.

With every gust, it twirled and spun,
Claiming it was always fun.
"I'm not just green, I'm delicate art!"
It boasted proudly with all its heart.

Yet when the winter cold did bite,
It whispered low, "Tonight, not right!"
Draped in frost, it shivered there,
While dreaming of the warm spring air.

With every season, moods will change,
In sunlight's warmth or chilly range.
The leaf still smiles, come what may,
In its own funny, leafy way.

The Language of Green Symphonies

In gardens where the creatures prance,
The leaves compose a leafy dance.
With rustling notes and colors bright,
They sing of joy from morn 'til night.

A beetle joins, a bug on bass,
It plays along with leafy grace.
They giggle tunes, a frolicking tune,
As crickets chirp beneath the moon.

The daisies nod as if to sway,
In perfect time with all the play.
While blooms, like flutes, add sweet allure,
In gardens grand, they feel so pure.

Thus sing they on, in vibrant green,
The quirkiest band you'd ever seen.
Together wrapped in laughter's gleam,
A symphony of nature's team.

Tales of Garden Whispers

In every nook, a secret brews,
Where daisies gossip and roses choose.
With petals pressed to share their fears,
They swap their jokes and shed their tears.

A worm once claimed he'd tell it best,
But tangled roots put him to rest.
The onions burped with smelly pride,
As green beans giggled, eyes opened wide.

The garden speaks in whispers low,
Of sunlit days and moonlight's glow.
A squirrel overhears with a wink,
Deciding it's all worth a drink.

So lift a cup in lively cheer,
To tales that bloom throughout the year.
For in this patch, the stories weave,
With laughter shared and none to grieve.

Chronicles of the Canopied Earth

In the jungle of dreams where shadows dance,
Leaves gossip in whispers, they take a chance.
A squirrel with style in a top hat grins,
While ants throw confetti as the party begins.

The branches are laughing, they sway with the breeze,
While flowers tell tales, oh, such funny degrees!
A parrot critiques in a posh accent swell,
As butterflies giggle, it's a wild stand-up spell.

Whispers of the Sylvan Paths

Along the leafy lanes where the critters convene,
A raccoon in a tux sings to a drum machine.
Pines are the audience, their needles on edge,
As the hedgehog breaks out in a soft, silly pledge.

The mushrooms are punchlines, sprouting with flair,
While daisies twirl whimsically in mid-air.
The roots crack up, they wiggle below,
In this forest of chuckles, the humor will grow.

The Pulse of Leaf and Stem

A stem with a heartbeat is quite the delight,
It dances at dusk, oh, what a strange sight!
Petals do pirouettes, a flower ballet,
While bees hold applause, buzzing their way.

With roots that have rhythm, they shake up the soil,
Each weed has a punchline, it's all in the toil.
Laughter erupts from the composted fears,
As the veggies tell jokes, we all lend them ears.

Echoes from the Garden's Edge

Near the fence where the weeds weave tales without end,
A cabbage confesses, it's lost a good friend.
The carrots are snickering, they hide from the sun,
While radishes poke fun, 'Are we the weird ones?'

The daisies declare it a flower furor,
As the onions cry laughter—don't ask for the cure!
The tomatoes roll over, they're ripe for a joke,
At the garden's edge, it's a backstage croak.

Emerald Canopy Whisper

In a room full of green, she quietly schemes,
A plant plots its role in her wildest dreams.
It sways side to side, with a cheeky grin,
Whispering secrets of where it's been.

Dust bunnies dance in the warm, bright light,
While soil gets festive, it's quite the sight.
She speaks to her leaves, they giggle and sway,
Telling tales of their adventures each day.

With sunlight as confetti, they twirl and bounce,
Leaves flapping wildly in rhythmic pounce.
Her worries dissolve like mist in the air,
This leafy ensemble beyond compare.

Overwatered or thirsty, they tease her so well,
Like a quirky sitcom, they raucously yell.
Embraced by the charm of this playful crew,
Who knew plant care could be such a hoot too!

Dappled Sunlight Serenade

In the corner it dances, so bold and so bright,
Under rays of the morning, what a delightful sight!
It waves like a flag, with a mischievous flair,
Singing songs of sunshine, filling up the air.

A sprinkle of water, a side sip of joy,
Each leaf is a laugh, a playful decoy.
Photosynthesis parties, they all come alive,
Shaking their stems, oh how they thrive!

The cat takes a leap, eyeing the show,
But those emerald dancers just steal the flow.
A dance-off begins, and they sway with delight,
Because in this green realm, it's a raucous night!

Her friends come to visit, the laughter does bloom,
They toast with their teas in this chlorophyll room.
Confessions of plants and their grand escapades,
In dappled sunlight, they throw their parades!

Leaves of a Wandering Heart

Oh, the tales these green pals would love to share,
Of journeys through jungles, and oh, the cool air!
From window to windowsill, they long to roam,
These leaf-spirited dreamers, calling plants their home.

One day they're low-key, just catching some light,
Next, they're on adventures, playing all night.
From kitchen to bathroom, a leafy escapade,
Swapping stories of places they've magically made.

Tall tales of glories and fronds filled with cheer,
Some leaves start to dance when the sun's drawing near.
With every new sprout, their laughter expands,
Who knew plant life could have such fun plans!

So here's to the leaves, with their wanderlust flair,
In the wild of her room, they frolic without care.
Their whispers will echo through each fleeting hour,
In the garden of giggles, they'll always have power!

Botanical Confessions

In the quiet of night, they giggle real loud,
Sharing secret confessions beneath the soft cloud.
Each leaf tells a story, where chaos ensued,
Mixing up their soil, oh what a rude brood!

"I swore I was a cactus!" one leafy bit laughed,
But lo and behold, it's a succulent craft!
Another sighs softly, "I thought I could sing,
Turns out I just rattle—such a silly thing!"

Fights over sunlight, the shadows comply,
As they reminisce on the times they could fly.
With each tiny hiccup, their roots intertwine,
In this world of green, they toast with some wine!

So heed their advice, dear plant-parent friend,
For even in silence, the fun doesn't end.
With each quirky quirk of their botanical play,
They teach us to cherish—even leaves have their day!

The Tapestry of Twisted Stems

In a pot that's far too small,
A plant stands proud but feels the wall.
Its leaves wave like they're in a band,
Twisting, turning, doing their stand.

They argue over sunlight's grace,
Finding drama in this small space.
With stems that dance a wobbly jig,
They plot their growth with silliness big.

A shadow here, a shadow there,
These leaves are plotting, oh beware!
Their nightly meetings, full of glee,
"Let's grow wild and carefree!"

So, if you see them wink and sway,
Just know they've had a fun-filled day.
With laughter shared through leafy dreams,
A pot of joy, or so it seems.

Folded Pages of Serenity

A plant that thinks it's reading books,
With leaves that curl and give right looks.
It flips a leaf like turning page,
In search of wisdom, quite the sage.

"Hello, my dear!" the fern does chime,
"Do you think we're wasting time?
These books have tales from far and wide,
But here we grow, with leafy pride!"

The sunlight spills like cup of tea,
As ferns debate their destiny.
With all this chatter, what a scene,
They sip the warmth, like it's cuisine.

So next time you feel quite alone,
Remember plants can make a home.
In folded pages, wisdom flows,
In all the laughter, life just glows.

Whispers Among the Leaves

In the quiet of the afternoon,
Leaves gossip softly, what a tune!
"Did you hear about the clumsy stem?
It tried to dance, fell on a gem!"

The ivy snickers, gives a shake,
"Here comes the breeze, a silly quake!"
With rustling voices, huddled tight,
They share their gossip, pure delight.

A leaf unveils a secret twist,
"Oh my goodness, you've missed missed!
The pot is empty, naked space,
We need more friends, a leafy place!"

So as they whisper, laugh, and sigh,
Remember plants have lives nearby.
With antics sprouting from each vein,
Their stories flutter, like a train.

A Portrait of Urban Greenery

In a city bustling, bright, and loud,
A cactus waves, "I'm quite proud!"
With sidewalk cracks as its fine art,
It grows defiantly, a leafy heart.

The potholes frown, "We're not your bed!"
But the cactus giggles, "You've been misled!"
With laughter blending with the cars,
It roots for life beneath the stars.

A fern peeks out from beneath a bench,
Wishing for sun, feeling quite drenched.
"Let's pop out next to that coffee shop,
Where smiles and laughter never stop!"

So when you stroll and gaze around,
Look for the leaves that laugh and bound.
In every corner, life does thrive,
A portrait where green feels so alive.

The Whispering Woods

In a forest full of trees,
Where branches tickle the knees,
Squirrels gossip with a tease,
And the leaves dance with ease.

A pine said, "I'm taller still,"
While oaks boast of their strong will,
But birches just take their chill,
In their white coats, oh what a thrill!

Rabbits hop around in glee,
Practicing their best ballet,
While a raccoon holds a spree,
Hosting parties by the bay.

In the woods, the jokes run free,
Who knew that trees could agree?
Laughter rustles through the spree,
Nature's giggles, can't you see?

Nature's Intricate Tapestry

A flower poked its head up high,
Said, "Watch me bloom, oh me, oh my!"
Nearby, a patch of weeds would sigh,
"We're just here to tell a lie!"

The daisies wrapped in bright attire,
Whispered secrets by the fire,
Joyfully they'd never tire,
As honeybees sang in choir.

A butterfly wearing specs so cool,
Claimed it ruled the garden school,
But caterpillars, with a drool,
Rolling eyes said, "What a fool!"

Nature weaves a tapestry,
Where giggles sway just like a spree,
Each petal holds a mystery,
And every bug a history!

Echoes in the Annual Rings

Year by year, the trees do speak,
Their rings reveal what's quite unique,
Some lived long, some felt the peak,
While others just found their hide-and-seek.

The maple shouts, "I gather sap!"
While birches chat, "Take a nap!"
Every year, with a happy clap,
They laugh at the annual mishap.

The winds carry tales so grand,
Of squirrels who stole the land,
Echoes sent from bark to sand,
Every laugh, a helping hand.

Each ring tells a story bright,
From sunny days to winter's bite,
In a dance of day and night,
The trees chuckle, oh what a sight!

Cadence of Chlorophyll

In a garden filled with green,
Where every leaf is like a queen,
Sunshine plays a lively scene,
And plants dance, oh so serene.

The ferns wave with gentle grace,
As the daisies join the race,
With ladybugs that spin and chase,
It's a cheeky, leafy place!

Roots tickle in the dark below,
While vines twist to and fro,
And ants march in hilarious show,
Always bustling, never slow.

Chlorophyll hums a tune so sweet,
In every leaf, it's a real treat,
Nature's rhythm, can't be beat,
A dance of life that's hard to cheat!

Messenger of the Verdant

In the corner sits a plant,
Waving leaves as if to chant.
Sunlight spills, a golden gift,
With every sway, my spirits lift.

It talks to me in leafy sighs,
Jokes about the sunlit skies.
A stand-up act, no pun intended,
With roots so deep, it's well grounded.

I pour some water, it quips with glee,
Telling tales of bees and tea.
Photosynthesis, the leafy dance,
It nudges me to join its prance.

So here we sit, a funny pair,
I sip my drink, it breathes the air.
A messenger from green domain,
In its humor, I lose all pain.

Elysian Fields of Flora

In a room where plants reside,
Every leaf is just my guide.
They whisper secrets, oh so sly,
Making me laugh, oh me, oh my!

One leaf said, 'I'm feeling fresh!'
While others blushed in leafy dress.
"Oh darling, don't be green with envy,
Join my reign, together we'd be trendy!"

A little pot of cactus grins,
Making jokes about its spines and sins.
In this realm of playful greens,
Laughter sprouts like vibrant beans.

Though we don't travel far and wide,
Our joy expands, it's like a tide.
With every chuckle, peace unfurls,
In these fields of funny curls.

Whispers of Green Shadows

In the shadows, green leaves sway,
Sharing jokes in a leafy way.
"Why so stiff?" the fern will tease,
"For a plant, can't you just feel ease?"

The pothos chuckles, hanging low,
Swaying gently to and fro.
"Don't take life too seriously,
Even roots can learn to be free!"

I sit beneath their playful song,
Wondering where the laughs belong.
Leaves giggle, do they have a clue?
That humor grows between us too!

In this green nook, oh what a sight,
Laughter dances in the light.
Join the party, hear the sound,
Whispers of joy forever abound.

Luminescent Leaves at Midnight

At midnight's hour, leaves gleam bright,
Like tiny stars in the silent night.
They gossip about what plants could do,
If they could wear shoes, or play peek-a-boo!

The succulents giggle, 'A tad too wet?'
While ferns flip leaves, a dance to beget.
'Hey, not too loud, we have our dreams!
At night, we plot and share our schemes.'

With a sprinkle of moonlight's glow,
Each leaf glimmers, starting the show.
They whisper 'puns' like seasoned pros,
Inviting me to join their throes.

So in this midnight green affair,
I find my joy and little care.
For in plant humor, life's delight,
Is wrapped in leaves that shine so bright.

The Hidden Life of Leaves

In the garden, they conspire,
Gossiping, they never tire.
Whispering tales of bees and bugs,
Throwing shade and sharing hugs.

When the wind begins to dance,
They shimmy off in leafy prance.
One, two, three, they start to tease,
Swaying gently in the breeze.

They plot and plan a leafy play,
Poking fun at drab, grey clay.
With every flutter, a laugh is sown,
In their world, we're just alone.

But when night falls, the fun is done,
They slip into dreams, just like the sun.
With twinkling stars above their heads,
They practice their jokes, tucked in their beds.

Secrets in the Sunlight

Sunny rays, they sit and chat,
Nibbling snacks — oh, imagine that!
One leaf whispers, 'I'm feeling fine!'
While another shouts, 'Where's the wine?'

With silly shadows prancing near,
They share their crush on a flower dear.
Petals blush, their gossip's bold,
In this radiant world, secrets unfold.

A raindrop's drip becomes a jest,
"Oh no!" they squeal, "We're in for a test!"
They smile and chuckle, shaking off dew,
'Cause in sunlight's warmth, they're just passing through.

As the daylight comes to a close,
They start to share who really knows.
Under moonlight's gentle plea,
The leaves giggle, staying carefree.

Lush Chronicles of Nature

In the wild, the leaves compete,
Showing off their vibrant sheet.
One says, "Look at this green sheen!"
Another boasts, "I'm the queen!"

With sunlight streaking through the trees,
They laugh and wink in playful tease.
A squirrel joins, with nuts in tow,
"Hey leaves, mind if I steal the show?"

The ants march on, a little parade,
While leaves make jokes, unafraid.
"Who's the tallest? Let's all compare!"
Giggles float, drifting on air.

But as dusk lingers, they settle down,
Under the stars, far from town.
They whisper dreams, with laughter rife,
In this jovial, leafy life.

Echoes of the Leafy Grove

In the grove where laughter rings,
Leaves clamor like they're magicians' things.
"Watch me twist, watch me spin!"
"Did you hear about my leafy grin?"

With every breeze, a rumor flies,
"Did you see those trees in disguise?"
The bark has tales of yore, it seems,
While leaves concoct the wildest dreams.

A game of hide and seek begins,
Daring games with playful grins.
But when it's time for the moon's embrace,
They settle in, a cozy space.

Tomorrow's sun gives promise bright,
To more frolics, fun, and light.
In leafy whispers, joy confides,
In nature's heart, laughter resides.

Melodies of the Growing Season

In a corner, a plant does sway,
Sunny laughter makes it play.
Leaves tap dance in morning light,
While soil giggles with delight.

Wind whirls in with a cheeky grin,
Rustling leaves like a violin.
Petals blush, they sway in tune,
Nature's prank beneath the moon.

Oh, the garden sings its song,
With critters dancing all night long.
In this patch of green delight,
Even weeds wear smiles so bright.

With every leaf and stem that climbs,
The world hums with silly rhymes.
As rains fall, they make a splash,
In this merry green bash!

Reflections in the Verdant Mirror

In shiny leaves, I see my face,
A big grin in this leafy place.
Mirrored joy in emerald sheen,
Who knew plants could be so keen?

Each droplet glints like a wink,
The pot seems to chuckle, don't you think?
With roots that tangle in the mud,
They giggle as they form a bud.

Life's a comedy just like a play,
Every sprout has something to say.
Fancy that, a fern with flair,
Sparkling humor fills the air!

So dance, laugh, and take a chance,
With leafy friends, we all can prance.
In this green realm where joy is clear,
The plants invite you to come near!

A Symphony of Chlorophyll

Chlorophyll orchestra on display,
Green maestro's in the fray.
Twigs and leaves scratch out a tune,
Swaying softly, over the moon!

The trumpet vine calls out loud,
While daisies form a giggling crowd.
A bass roar comes from the tree,
As squirrels strum a symphony!

Harmony found in every branch,
With pollinators ready to dance.
Buzzing notes swept through the field,
To nature's whims, we all must yield.

In this anthem of the green,
Where joy is simple and serene,
Even weeds join the grand affair,
With laughter soaring through the air!

The Artistry of Petiole and Blade

Petiole and blade in a clever art,
They paint a canvas that warms the heart.
Curly leaves in a funky twist,
Creativity in nature's midst!

A leaf rolls up, strikes a pose,
While nearby sprout shows off its clothes.
Colors splash like a painter's spree,
Who knew green could be so free?

With every angle, they turn and sway,
Making sure to have their say.
In this garden, giggles bloom,
As joy erupts, filling the room!

So marvel at their daring style,
And let their laughter make you smile.
For in this realm of vibrant green,
Artistry and fun are always seen!

In the Green Embrace

In a pot where leaves do sway,
A plant thinks it's the star of the day.
It poses proud, just soaking sun,
Saying, 'Hey world, I'm the number one!'

The cat walks by with a knowing smirk,
As if to say, 'You're just a big jerk!'
But green friend hums a leafy tune,
Dreaming of fame, perhaps a monsoon.

But when the rain pours down in sheets,
Our leafy friend just admits defeat.
With soggy roots and a droopy frown,
It shouts, 'This weather is bringing me down!'

Then comes the sun with a bright smile,
Warming the leaves, oh what a style!
A dance begins with a gentle breeze,
The plant, once moody, is now at ease.

Tales from the Leafy Realm

In a home full of quirky greens,
Each leaf tells tales from unseen scenes.
One leaf whispers, 'I had a fright,
A sneaky dust bunny snuck in last night!'

Another chimes in with a giggle,
'Our pot's just become a jiggle wiggle!'
They shake and shiver, but hold on tight,
As the cat leaps through in a silly sight.

'Oh let's not fight, let's laugh instead,
Before the sunlight puts us to bed!'
So they giggle, twist, and play along,
Creating a chorus, a leafy song.

In this realm where the silly grows,
Each leaf knows well how the humor flows.
With every turn and every twist,
They learn that laughter can't be missed!

Shadows of Verdant Dreams

In shadows cast by leaf and stem,
A world awakens, an odd little gem.
Where bugs debate on who reigns supreme,
And plant pots host a nighttime dream.

Mossy whispers, secrets unfold,
As night bugs gather, feeling bold.
One boasts loudly, 'I'm the best flyer!'
While another laughs, 'I'm a leaf's liar!'

A glow worm glows with a dancer's grace,
Sashaying through this bug-filled space.
'Join the party!' it claims, bright and keen,
As shadows dance to the moon's sheen.

Yet as dawn breaks, they scatter and flee,
Back to their homes, oh where could they be?
Our leafy friends with a teary goodbye,
Say, 'See you tonight, under the sky!'

A Symphony of Fronds

In a room filled with a leafy crowd,
Fronds sway gently, feeling quite proud.
Each leaf plays its part with flair,
Creating a symphony, light as air.

The cat taps a rhythm with soft little paws,
While plants join in with their leafy applause:
'Add a twist here and a turn there,' they say,
Making music that brightens the day.

A watering can joins with a clink and a splash,
As drops fall down, oh what a bash!
The soil hums low, a bass so deep,
While junk on the floor takes a daring leap.

But as the finale draws near with grace,
Leaves tousle, twist, and find their place.
A concert of nature, both wild and free,
In a world where even plants like to be!

Leaves as Lighthouses

In a room full of green, they stand tall,
Shining bright, like guides to us all.
With fluttering tips, they dance in delight,
Casting shadows that tickle the night.

They lean a bit left and then to the right,
Checking the wall as if plotting a flight.
Each crinkle and fold, a secret to share,
With whispers they've heard from the sun in the air.

When light comes to play, oh what a show,
They wave and they wiggle, putting on a glow.
A lopsided grin on every broad leaf,
A leafy parade of joy and belief.

So here's to the leaves, those lighthouses green,
Holding stories of giggles just waiting to glean.
In pot or in plot, they humor us all,
A whimsical crew, keeping spirits enthralled.

Unraveling the Leafy Layers

Peel back the layers, what do we find?
A comedy show where the roots unwind.
With each wrinkled edge, a tale to unfold,
Of leaf gossip sessions, and seeds that are bold.

A leaf with a wink and a cheeky little curl,
Tells tales of the cat that gave it a twirl.
In sunshine's embrace, they plot and they scheme,
Dreaming of leaf biscuits, and leaf-shaped ice cream.

Underneath those layers, don't be surprised,
Are jokes about beetles, both wise and unwise.
A chorus of green laughter, who'd ever believe?
That plants have their secrets, so much up their sleeve!

So dive into green, let your worries unfurl,
In the world of the leaves, let imaginations swirl.
With each leafy layer, the fun will begin,
Unraveling joy with a broad leafy grin.

Mood Swings of the Green Realm

Oh the mood swings of green, what a sight to behold,
One minute they're cheerful, the next, they're cold.
A sunny, beaming jade in the morning light,
By noon, a sulker, pretending to fight.

They sway with the breeze, like a dance in the sun,
Then droop like a sleepyhead, claiming it's done.
"Water me, please!" they dramatically cry,
While secretly loving the attention nearby.

With a frown, they proclaim they've got needs to express,
Then beam like a star, when the care's at its best.
From sparkly to silly, their antics astound,
In the vibrant green realm, laughter abounds.

So watch for the signals when their moods start to shift,
Join in their fun, and share in their gift.
For in every curl and in every swoon,
Are the giggles and wiggles of a leafy cartoon.

The Story Beneath the Soil

Beneath all that green, oh what a tale,
Of roots mingling joyfully, a leafy cartel.
They whisper and giggle, in dark, cozy beds,
Planning great adventures with tricks on their heads.

"Let's trip up that squirrel!" one root said with glee,
"Or lure in the rain, just wait and you'll see!"
They shimmy and shake, with a soil-filled cheer,
The stories below, oh, they're always near.

With worms as their audience, they put on a show,
About dance parties held, where no one can go.
Dirt is their dance floor, a comical stage,
As roots leap about with exuberant rage.

So let's raise a toast to the fun 'neath the ground,
Where roots knit together, joyfully bound.
For the tales underground, though hidden from view,
Bring laughter to life, if you only knew!

The Soul of the Garden

In a patch of soil, they gather round,
Blades of grass gossip, no sound profound.
Rosemary winks at the carrots' plight,
Singing of sunshine, bantering light.

Worms tell tales of muddy delight,
While daisies dance in their floral flight.
Chase away pests with laughter so bold,
For secrets of joy in blooms unfold.

Potted plants plot in quirky disguise,
Trading their stories beneath the skies.
With every rustle, a chuckle is heard,
Nature's own whispers, utterly absurd.

They banter with bees, in pollen they dive,
Those funny little critters, somehow alive!
Gardens, a circus of green and delight,
Where the plants all hold court under moonlight.

Symphony of the Shadows

The sun dips low, the shadows grow tall,
Lurking like whispers, they dance through the hall.
Crickets are tuning their tiny stringed shows,
While moles critique, sharing murmurs and prose.

Under the moon, the gnomes take the stage,
In a comical play, they're all filled with rage.
Squirrels audition, their leaps oh so grand,
But the shadow puppets steal the show on demand.

The leaves rustle softly, a gentle applause,
For the vines that are stretching with no hint of pause.
Each shadow a story, a flicker of fun,
They all bow together, the day is now done.

Laughter resounds in this playful charade,
As the stars wink knowingly, unafraid.
A symphony sweet, with a mischievous blend,
The night is alive, may the giggles extend.

Slices of Emerald

Lettuce romps in the salad parade,
Cucumbers sly, in the coolness displayed.
Tomatoes giggle, so plump and so red,
While avocados dream in their buttery bed.

Radishes wear crowns, in their spiky delight,
Zucchini's a jester, a marvelous sight.
Peppers play hide and seek under the sun,
Each slice a riddle, oh, this is such fun!

Herbs throw confetti, basil's the king,
With rosemary tunes, they begin to sing.
Join in the frolic, it's veggie ballet,
As flora creates art in its own quirky way.

Laugh with the onions, each tear a good jest,
While corn on the cob thinks it's simply the best.
A feast full of laughter, a garden so bright,
Colorful, witty, under soft starlight.

Stories from the Green Abyss

In nooks of the garden, secrets reside,
Frogs croak out stories, their eyes opened wide.
Lizards are lurking, with sly little grins,
As the tales of the night begin to spin.

With vines and tendrils, they weave through the air,
Whispering shenanigans rooted with care.
Slugs are the poets, with slimy quills bright,
Crafting their verses in the shade of the night.

Dewdrops are diamonds, their laughter like chimes,
While beetles proclaim their funny old rhymes.
Every critter chiming in with delight,
In the depths of the garden, a comical sight.

So listen intently, there's magic at play,
For in every leaf, a tale's on display.
The green abyss chuckles, secrets unfurled,
A humorous realm, a whimsical world.

The Language of Leaf and Light

In sunlit chatter, leaves do sway,
They gossip softly, come what may.
A swirling breeze brings whispers near,
As plants share secrets, weird but dear.

With sunlight's touch, they spread delight,
In shades of green, they dance in sight.
Photosynthesis, a leafy dream,
In this grand play, they steal the scene.

They pop and crackle, voices bold,
Tales of rain, and sunbeam gold.
Oh, how they laugh at wind's embrace,
Nature's humor in leafy space.

So listen close to nature's choir,
Each leaf a note in green attire.
In this green world, so alive,
The language of leaves will always thrive.

Enigmas in the Jungle

In the jungle where shadows loom,
Lies a riddle of leaves with a sense of gloom.
Why do monkeys wear hats so neat?
It's their cover for the pizza feast!

Vines twist like spaghetti high,
Chasing after the clouds in the sky.
Lizards wearing sunglasses so cool,
Say, 'Watch out! This is our swimming pool!'

Frogs in tuxedos play piano tunes,
While turkeys dance beneath the moons.
In a world where whimsy thrives,
Every creature has a laugh that jives.

So wander deep where secrets dwell,
In the jungle's heart, there's always a spell.
With every step, a giggle's grown,
In the land of puzzles, we're never alone.

Roots Beneath the Surface

Down where the roots tickle the ground,
A party's happening, without a sound.
Worms in tuxes, dancing all night,
Throwing a bash that feels just right.

They twist and turn in a wiggly way,
With beetles clapping to the display.
A fungal DJ spins a track,
While tiny ants keep bringing snacks.

All the creatures join in the fun,
In a hidden world, where all's well done.
So dive below, don't be shy,
Join the rooty revelry, oh my!

For what seems still above the grass,
Is a wild disco, don't let it pass.
With every thump of the underground beat,
You'll find this party can't be beat!

The Green Sonnet

Oh, leafy friends with your mighty grace,
In your green embrace, the world's a race.
Photosynthetic silliness widespread,
Under your watch, all worries shed.

You sway and jiggle in a playful breeze,
Tickling the trees, oh how they tease!
From perched birds to ants on parade,
In this jolly realm, no plans need made.

Each leaf's a joker, full of surprise,
With swaying stems and wandering eyes.
Nature's laughter fills the air,
In this green laughter, there's love to share.

So let's rejoice, in this verdant spree,
Where banter blooms and hearts run free.
For in the garden of life's own chat,
Humor's the magic, imagine that!

A Study in Leafy Layers

In a pot so grand, a leaf stands still,
With dreams of dancing on a windowsill.
It wiggles and jives, trying to impress,
While ignoring the dust on its leafy dress.

A friend once claimed it could sing a tune,
Under the glow of a full-blown moon.
But alas, it hums a dull, green song,
As folks raise brows and ask, "What's wrong?"

Each morning, it stretches, reaches for light,
Wishing for cloud nine, but lands in a plight.
With squirrels watching, it starts to sway,
You'd think it's auditioning for Broadway!

Oh, leafy friend, in your pot so comfy,
You spin tales of laughter, all soft and fluffy.
Though rooted quite firm, you dream and you flare,
In your green little world, we banish despair.

Where Flora Meets Fantasy

Once met a plant with quite the flair,
Claiming to waltz with the unicorn's hair.
With costumes of moss, it puts on a show,
While neighbors just wonder, "Where did it go?"

It twirls through the night, casting shadows so wild,
One leaf upright, surely a mischief-filled child.
With whispers of petals, it shares secret dreams,
Of tea parties hosted with moonlight and beams.

When sunlight arrives, it's a sly little prank,
Hiding its tricks with a wink and a flank.
While daisies judge from their sunny parade,
This rogue little leaf just laughs and displays.

At dusk, it prepares for the nighttime so bright,
Setting the stage for its leafy delight.
For wherever it grows, there's humor and jest,
Just a plant with a heart, on a whimsical quest.

Botanical Reveries in Moonlight

In slumber, the leaves weave stories of cheer,
Of wandering vines that dance without fear.
Under the gaze of the shimmering star,
They giggle at pots that seem oh-so bizarre.

Oh, how they dream of patches and earth,
Imagining parties, full of mirth.
The soil chats back with a nutty old tale,
Of cactus conquests and fungal detail.

With moonlight as host, a gathering grows,
With wildflower gossip that everyone knows.
They swap their best secrets, a leafy affair,
While neighbors roll eyes, breathing garden air.

A cosmos of plants in the mellow moon's glow,
Creating old legends that nobody knows.
So here's to the leaves in their moonlit soft flight,
Sipping on laughter deep into the night.

The Harmony of Growth

In a garden of giggles, the seedlings aspire,
Growing together, they set hearts on fire.
With roots intertwined, a glorious dance,
These botanicals surely took chance.

Potatoes wear shades, finding sun's good side,
While radishes gossip and secretly bide.
The strawberries blush, so timid and red,
As daisies declare, "What's the news?" they said.

With laughter like breezes that tickle and sway,
The radish retorts, "I won't live in dismay!"
While beans in a row try their best to compete,
In a race for the sun, finished with a beat.

And thus, in this patch, where joy tends to sprout,
Harmony reigns, laughing through the drought.
A circus of growth, in a leafy domain,
What fun will they conjure, come sunshine or rain?

The Joy of Botanical Charms

In the corner stands a green delight,
With leaves that dance in morning light.
I water it daily, sing songs of cheer,
Hoping it knows I'm always near.

Its roots tickle dirt like a playful friend,
Plant mischief, the garden's latest trend.
Should I talk to it in a silly voice?
Or just let it grow, without much choice?

Each leaf a hand, with fingers wide,
Telling me secrets the soil can hide.
I'll dress it up in ribbons and bows,
For plant fashion shows, who really knows?

So here's to plants, our quirky pals,
With stories of bugs and leafy pals.
We'll giggle together, share all our dreams,
Living in a world of botanical themes.

Kaleidoscope of Growth

In my sunny nook, a leaf parade,
With colors bright, nothing will fade.
Each sprout appears like a joyful surprise,
A garden of laughter right before my eyes.

One leaf is shy, another's quite bold,
Their little antics never get old.
Do they gossip when I'm not around?
I'd love to know what they say on the ground!

A twist and a turn, the stems do sway,
Twirling to life in a plant cabaret.
I toss them some soil, they dance with glee,
In this leafy circus, it's just them and me.

So here's to the green, quirky and spry,
Their jovial vibes lift spirits up high.
Together we flourish, a botanical crew,
In a kaleidoscope world that feels ever new.

Rustle Underfoot

Walking through green, a soft rustle calls,
It's just my plants, making leafy brawls.
Each step is met with a playful plea,
As they whisper to me, 'Hey, look at me!'

A leaf nods hello, while another plays shy,
They seem to know my every sigh.
Do they plot when I'm not in sight?
Creating chaos, just for delight?

With every footfall, there's a story to share,
Of hidden bug dances and sunbeam flair.
Watch out for soil bombs when I make a trip,
My botanical pals launch a friendly quip.

So tread with care, through this green delight,
Where laughter and joy take glorious flight.
The rustle underfoot, a symphony true,
In the secretive world of leaf and dew.

The Journey of Sap and Soil

In the depths of earth, a whispered quest,
Tiny roots stir, seeking the best.
They stumble through darkness, a narrow lane,
On a wobbly path like an ink-stained train.

Sap journeys up like a cheerful sprite,
Tickling leaves in the soft daylight.
What do they chat about, up so high?
"Hey, check the clouds! They look rather spry!"

Mischievous, they bask in the sun's glow,
With a leafy giggle, they steal the show.
Can a plant laugh, if no one is near?
Oh, believe me, they play overtly clear!

And so they rise on their leafy spree,
A party of green, oh what glee!
From deep in the soil to the sky's grand swirl,
The journey unfolds in this botanical whirl.

www.ingramcontent.com/pod-product-compliance
Lightning Source LLC
Chambersburg PA
CBHW070317120526
44590CB00017B/2719